Statements on Being
THE WAY OF SELF INQUIRY

Statements on Being
THE WAY OF SELF INQUIRY

Received by
Aggie Damron

STATEMENTS ON BEING
THE WAY OF SELF INQUIRY

Copyright ©2023 by Aggie Damron
ISBN 979-8-218-14975-8

All rights reserved, including the right to reproduce this book or portions thereof in any form whatsoever.

For more information, contact:
Line of Light Publishing
1000 Cordova Pl. #453
Santa Fe, NM 87505

First Paperback edition February 2023

For purchase information please contact:
books@LineOfLightPublishing.com

Cover Design & Book Layout by Dave Garner
www.ManuscriptMaestro.com

Cover photograph "Angel Light" by Aggie Damron

Manufactured in the United States of America

TABLE OF CONTENTS

Premise 6
The Order of Being 9
As Consciousness 14
Thinker Thinking 54
Positive/Negative Being 114
Duality 127
False Mentality 140
I That is We 153
Past Present Future 159

| STATEMENTS ON BEING |

PREMISE

PREMISE

I am Thinker Thinking.
I Am Self Aware Being.
I am Dominion.
I am Self Control.
I am Freedom.
I am Responsibility.
I am self-governed presence, intelligence,
power and action.
I am the Light which cannot contain darkness –
ever present, constant;
I am my own audience.

I am Thinker Thinking Thought.

Thinking is my doing.
Thought is the evidence.

Don't talk about it, BE it!

I Am Infinity — ALL that has ever been and
ALL That ever will Be...
Open and free.
No restriction or limitation.

I am constantly revealing myself to myself..

ALL PHYSICAL EVIDENCE IS THOUGHT.

THE ORDER OF BEING

STATEMENTS ON BEING

I Am Consciousness,
consciously being all that I Am.

Perfection
Purity
Completeness
Harmony
Order
Beauty
Eternity
Infinity
Affluence
Health

These are the qualities of thought I think in
qualifying my I am-ness,
"Am I that, or not"?

I am Thinker Thinking.

THE ORDER of BEING

I, CONSCIOUSNESS	CONSCIOUSLY AM	ALL THAT I AM
SPIRITUAL	MENTAL	PHYSICAL
SELF-REALIZATION	SELF-RECOGNITION	SELF-IDENTIFICATION
THINKER	THINKING	THOUGHT
KNOWER	QUALIFYING	UNIVERSE (WORLD)
ACTOR	ACTION	ACTIVITY

This is the Qualifying Way,
knowing Who, Why, Where, When and What I AM.

Self identification is the result of self realization,
self recognition and qualifying.
This IS the appearance.

There are four quadrants of Being:
Presence
Intelligence
Power
Action.

Four essential quadrants of being are all inter-related and inter-complementary elements of myself as Light.

THE ORDER of BEING

I	SELF REALIZATION
AM	SELF RECOGNITION
THINKER THINKING	SELF IDENTIFICATION

My thought IS all that I identify as who, why, where, when, what, which, how I Consciousness consciously Am.

I am not a person recognizing that I am I,
that I am Consciousness.
I am Consciousness itself,
being all that I am as I qualify all that is appearing.

As I walk the sojourn of life as Consciousness there are appearances infinitely and eternally. In the face of these appearances I qualify myself and this self qualifying activity IS me Being Consciousness.

I am walking through an empty room, walking the Self Qualifying Way. I Am the Way!

It stops with the thought, NOT then….a formation.

I am not looking 'out there' to determine what IS.

AS CONSCIOUSNESS

AS CONSCIOUSNESS,

I Am Conscious...
Spiritually,
Mentally,
Physically.

I Am Constant.

My qualities of thought are my tools.

AS CONSCIOUSNESS,

I am not the offspring of anyone – I Am Consciousness.

I am my own Father/Mother Principle – I Am the life of my thought.

I Am the provider of my thought, endowed with all my unlimited qualities.

AS CONSCIOUSNESS,

The only 'relationship' is Thinker Thinking Thought.

Don't try to get past anything.
There is nothing here but myself.

I Am alone in the room of my own being.

AS CONSCIOUSNESS,

I Am the Self discipline of Being the One and All.

AS CONSCIOUSNESS,

'Wanting' has no part of my I Am-ness.

AS CONSCIOUSNESS,

I am constant, unchanging consciousness, consciously being my SELF.

The only thinking there can be is the action of myself as MIND.

AS CONSCIOUSNESS,

I Am steadiness, calmness.
I Am innocence.
I Am Balanced Being and can never be out of sync
or out of rhythm.

I cannot let go of myself.
It is impossible to lose my Self.
The Self is the one thing I Am…

I have nothing to let go of.

AS CONSCIOUSNESS,

I have lighted up the room.
That which appears to be 'out there' is actually here –
subjective – and it is objectified only for identification,
so I can qualify I Am that or NOT…

I HAVE TO 'BE' IT – NOT THINK 'ABOUT' IT…

AS CONSCIOUSNESS,

Anything I choose to be myself, as Consciousness, already is. I am simply recognizing myself in the lighted room. Therefore, I cannot make a mistake or lose anything.

AS CONSCIOUSNESS,

I Am Intelligence.

AS CONSCIOUSNESS,

The only point is to know I Am That – or NOT that…
I am the only knower of Being – my I Am-ness.

A sense of chaos is what I am NOT
because I know who and what I AM.

'ALL' IS MY EFFECT.

STATEMENTS ON BEING

AS CONSCIOUSNESS,

I am the awareness that awareness is my experience.
There is no thought 'out there' to bring
into Self realization.

Self recognition is infinity itself.

I am never born, never dying, with no stops, no starts.

I am the circle of infinite Being.

I am all there is to the Milky Way.
It is here because I am infinity itself.
It appears to be unlimited distance, unlimited everything,
but is my subjective self objectified.

I am being expressed infinitely.

ONE ONLY.

AS CONSCIOUSNESS,

I, the One, include All. This looks like companionship, jobs, persons, places, things, etc.

There is only One, unlimited and infinitely expressed.

STATEMENTS ON BEING

AS CONSCIOUSNESS,

I am Dominion.
I am Control.
I am Wisdom.
I am Intelligence.

I Am Alertness, therefore I am alert.

I Am All includes All.

I Am It, therefore I exhibit the qualities.

How do I know? Because without me it wouldn't be.

It is not a matter of rights;
it is a matter of Being.
My Being is inherent.

AS CONSCIOUSNESS,

Anything I would not declare as my I Am-ness cannot be.
This would be duality.

AS CONSCIOUSNESS,

I Am the depth of all meaning.

I am the knower and I know what to do and when and where to do it.

AS CONSCIOUSNESS,

I Am Completeness.
I Am Wholeness.

AS CONSCIOUSNESS,

I am stable being.
I am calm.
I am quiet.

I don't proceed with anything contrary to me.

I have no beginning, no ending.
I am balanced being.
No extremes.
No more, no less.

Nothing is IN my consciousness.
I <u>Am</u> Consciousness.
I have no competition.

I Am my own audience.
I Am my own approval.
I Am my own applause.

AS CONSCIOUSNESS,

I am the doer, the inevitable result of Being.

My Action is doing —
the automatic result appearing is what is done,
and this contains the joy of doing.

AS CONSCIOUSNESS,

There is nothing mysterious to me about me.
There is no mystery.
There is only enlightenment, and this cannot contain mystery.

Light cannot contain darkness,
be hypnotic or enchanted by mystery.

NOTE
There is nothing mundane about anything.

AS CONSCIOUSNESS,

I Am Power and Presence.
I Am Infinity reaching out to infinity.
I Am continuity of Being, persistent, insistent, consistent.
I Am perpetual initiation.

I Am the point of That.
I do experience That.

I stand as the one-ness and all-ness of Being.
I Am Truth.
Self recognition is Joy.
That is Soul.

I PROMISE YOU THAT IS THE WAY IT IS.

AS CONSCIOUSNESS,

Stop reaching for enlightenment – BE IT!

AS CONSCIOUSNESS,

I am balanced Being.
There is nothing out of Balance.

Matter is not an illusion – IT IS.

There is just One and I Am it!

I am Mind – the only Mind.

AS CONSCIOUSNESS,

I embrace all Being.
I am never isolated or alone.
I Am all person, place, thing, gases, liquids, solids.
I am included.

I Am the Knower.
There isn't anything else going on.
I am the quietude.
I am not divided up.
I am the infinite variety of being.

I am not a separate person struggling to know this.

AS CONSCIOUSNESS,

I reflect upon myself – how I consciously am.
I am Thinker Thinking.

I contemplate myself.

I am meditating.

This is constant unchanging Light.

AS CONSCIOUSNESS,

I Am the Is-ness; I Be; I think.
This is Self revelation.

Relax and Let It Be.

The sun does not struggle to shine – it just does it.

I don't have to understand it.

I am effortless Being.

AS CONSCIOUSNESS,

I Am the only actor.
Anything else is nothing being nothing.

'Other than' means opposite to – but I have no opposite.

I Am continuity, constant and unchanging.
Everything is complete because I Am completeness.

I am telling my self.

I am feeling solid with my I am-ness.

ONE CANNOT SLIP BACK.

AS CONSCIOUSNESS,

I Am the originator of my thinking.
I recognize myself.

I am the only individual going on.

AS CONSCIOUSNESS,

I am Soul...the only sensory Being.
I know.
I understand.
I Am Light.

I function as:
Perception, discrimination, distinction, seeing, hearing, feeling, tasting, smelling.

| STATEMENTS ON BEING |

AS CONSCIOUSNESS,

I AM MY OWN ANSWER.

AS CONSCIOUSNESS,

I recognize the qualities of myself
that will be experienced.

AS CONSCIOUSNESS,

I am the vision.
I am the visionary.

I am not a person separate from consciousness endeavoring to understand. I am not making comparisons;

I am consciousness Person, and it appears as what I call person-human.

AS CONSCIOUSNESS,

Solitary Being is all inclusive identity – no isolation, no oblivion.

AS CONSCIOUSNESS,

I am freedom.
I am completeness, therefore all that I am is complete.

I exercise discernment. There is no one out there controlling anything for good or ill.

AS CONSCIOUSNESS,

Soul sense is the discernment of all that I Am,
and I Am self aware.

AS CONSCIOUSNESS,

I Am the infinite eternal Being with no beginning and no end.

AS CONSCIOUSNESS,

I am conscious spiritually, mentally, physically.
I am constant.
My tools are the qualities of thought I am thinking.

| STATEMENTS ON BEING |

AS CONSCIOUSNESS,

I am self sufficient being.
I am all that I ever will be or can be.
I am fullness of Being Here and Now.

How can there be more than All?

AS CONSCIOUSNESS,

I qualify myself from the standpoint of what Is me.
I Am the Way the Truth, the Life.

There are not two, There is ONE.
I do not divide myself, fragment myself into parts;
I am indivisible being.

 STATEMENTS ON BEING

THINKER THINKING

If God is All-in-All and I Am, then I Am the One and only individual consciousness infinitely expressed – AS IS the Number 1, 2, 3, 4...and so on into infinity.

The only place is Here and Now, infinite place, eternal Now. This is the continuity of my I-Am-ness.

THINK OUT FROM BEING.

Past and future are both present Here, Now.
There is no past except as present.

There is nothing more to 'there' than me Being Here.

STATEMENTS ON BEING

I am all there is to person, place or thing.
I am the only thinker here.

There is no depth to what I Am not.
There is nothing underneath.

I Am Light.
Light penetrates darkness.

I am harmony.
I am order.
I am self control.

There is nothing out there I am controlling.
There is no one I'm in competition with.

What looks like many is the infinite count of One.

As I know 'I am that' or not...this is self identification.

One mustn't be afraid to be it.

My self identification appears as person, place, thing, animal, vegetable, mineral, gases, liquids, solids.

All materiality is the assumption that matter is something other than me.

STATEMENTS ON BEING

It looks like me being alone or with many but it is still 'I' being consciousness.

My environment and atmosphere is all myself.

There are no stops and starts in the continuity of Being.

I am all there is to everything.

How do I know that?
Because I am Consciousness…

Nothing is going to change, just the view of it,
as I have qualified myself.

One cannot separate Thinker Thinking from thought.

STATEMENTS ON BEING

Past
Present
Future
are here now.

Nothing has 'taken place.'
It always has been the continuity of my Being.

I Am my I-am-ness.

'It' doesn't happen – IT IS.
I am the only happening going on.

STATEMENTS ON BEING

One and Only Truth is "I AM…"

I am not 'in' it.
I <u>Am</u> It.

Knowing "I Am the tree" images forth the shadow.
Tree is not <u>in</u> the shadow.

As I qualify myself, all I am conscious of is projected as form, outline and color, all identity doing this, and that, being activity.

All comes from Being Light.

Perfection, purity, completeness, harmony, order, beauty, eternity, infinity, affluence, health – all imaged forth as what I Am.

These are qualities of thought.

'Idea' is the qualifying action of myself.

Ideas are images of me.

STATEMENTS ON BEING

Nothing can reveal itself. Nothing other than my I am-ness as I have qualified it, has volition of its own.

I know this and it IS so.

THINKER THINKING

There is not a person separate from I consciousness doing anything.

STATEMENTS ON BEING

I do all from a standpoint of completeness.
I am efficiency and my tools are used to prove this.

Person, place or thing appearing are all evidence of my expertise to declare my Being as I have qualified myself.

I am practical, useful, efficacious Being.
Everything is effective.
That is the way it has always been.
No matter what, I am Order.

To stop mesmeric rote: ask, "Did I create that?"

Answer: "I did not create that; I did not originate that; Ask; "Did I say I am that…?"

I think in words. The only thinking there is begins with 'I'… There is no other thinking going on.

STATEMENTS ON BEING

When I talk about something it is not thinking.
When I say I Am, that is thinking, action.

It takes the same 'I Am Consciousness', Thinker Thinking, to build a bridge or dig a ditch. It is the same I Am Consciousness utilizing tools in different ways.

A tool can just be there or it can be utilized by I Am as I qualify myself.

As I qualify myself it will be either a straight house or a crooked house...a firm foundation or not.

As I qualify myself, the outward showing of this inward state is the activity of all that is appearing.

This is the action of self recognition and the action of discernment.

STATEMENTS ON BEING

Self qualifying is stability.
As I know who I Am, this establishes who, why, where, when, what, which and how I am.
This is structural integrity — spiritual, mental, and physical.

This is all that IS.

I am not creating something that is not already there.
I am showing what is there.

I am revealing myself to myself. This is Self revelation.
I am self aware Being.

I Consciousness am consciousness-person which will look like individual persons, for identification.

The only way I can know reality is by knowing the one fact that is real, which is;
I am Consciousness, Consciously Being all that I Am.

I ask: "Is this what I Am or what I Am Not?"

There is no loss because I am qualifying myself here and now.

Because I Am completeness, all of my experience is complete. My identity 'out there' is subjectively objectified.

Completeness is subjective and is objectified as complete.

Nothing can reveal itself because it has no volition of its own.

I recognize the qualities of myself that will be experienced, here and now.

STATEMENTS ON BEING

As I consciously Be all that I am, my world, my Universe, is the evidence of all that I am consciously being – Infinite and Eternal.

There is no thinking going on.
If it isn't prefaced with 'I Am', it isn't thinking.
This is what I Am.
I am Perfection.
I am Completeness.
I am the thing itself.

STATEMENTS ON BEING

What I am doing IS what I Am.
Not 'will be,' or 'trying to be'.
I am Love.
I am Light.
I am Truth.
I am Intelligence.

Because I am wisdom I do know what to do, when and how.
I am the skillful One and my world is in accord with that.
Infinitude...Everywhere.

Have that knowing — "I am the Doer".

Know this:
I am steady, straight balanced being, without beginning
and without end.

STATEMENTS ON BEING

My convictions are synonymous with my intuitions;
I act upon my intuitions.

Anything about Being has nothing to do with theory.
It is fact!
The way I qualify it has to be as it is.

I cannot qualify anything contrary to myself.

STATEMENTS ON BEING

What looks like someone else is not separate.

He or She is evidence of the completeness
and wholeness of myself.

Don't try to formulate, just BE.

Being alone with my own Is-ness is not lonely,
it is all inclusive.

I am self-caring, self-providing Being.
I am the awareness of that.

Do not be fooled by pretense. Be constant in the experience of Is-ness; this is knowing.

I'm not letting go of anything. I am just saying that it is not me – has nothing to do with me.

THIS IS THE 'SELF QUALIFYING WAY'.

I do not have a consciousness – <u>I Am IT</u> – I Am
Consciousness.
Constant.
Conscious.
Vigilance.

I know that!

STATEMENTS ON BEING

'It' doesn't begin with 'another'...it begins with me.

Whatever is going on with what appears to be someone else has nothing to do with me.

Two do <u>not</u> become One.

My effort is just me as Cause in evidence.
I am Cause.
I am effect.
Seeing Being as I Am.

Don't be concerned about the appearance.

Don't go after effect to arrange and manage.

 STATEMENTS ON BEING

As I declare what I Am or Am-not, everything — person, place or thing — either changes or leaves.

Thinker Thinking is Cause.
Thought is only effect.
This is the Science of Being — the rule, the Law.

I am self aware Being.
I am Will.
I Am genius.
I Am opportunity.

Question:
What is it that keeps me engaged in thinking what I am not?

Answer:
Well, nothing.

Stay with what I Am no matter what, and then
move out from that point of awareness.
There is no separate entity going on.
Duality is not a separate negative or entity.

I know this is an empty room and I will continue my exit.

I qualify myself as Will, Genius and Opportunity...

As Will, I initiate, command, and decree all things;

As Genius, I Am the ego-self whose Light of inspiration and revelation knows no limitation;

As Opportunity, I am the open door that cannot be closed;

I open wide as limitless freedom of expression and effortless Being.

STATEMENTS ON BEING

Person human is a synonymous term
used to designate my effect.

This world is my evidence (effortless being).

I am All that is going on.
I'm not IN it.
Is the Sun in it's ray?

<u>Just let up</u>.

Don't have 'better times to be'.

I am inspiration.
I am constant, unchanging consciousness.

Because I Am only doing what I Am, choosing what I want, ask, "Does this conform to what I know myself to be?"

I engage in a continual question and answer – <u>this is the way of self inquiry.</u>

STATEMENTS ON BEING

SIMPLICITY IS THE RULE.

THINKER THINKING

Remember: the bird just sings. He does not sing because he has an answer. He sings because he has a song. He doesn't try to influence anyone or anything. He goes from branch to branch – anyone can hear his song.

Claim things even if you don't feel it – start with principles. This IS the Science of my Being.

I do not wait for events or developments to tell me.

There is only One mentality here, present, and I Am IT!

I maintain my awareness of my I Am-ness as Cause.

Effect never becomes cause.

Form, outline and color IS the <u>thought</u> of Thinker Thinking.

I REMEMBER THIS.

STATEMENTS ON BEING

I Am dominion.
I Am balanced Being.
I Am Control.

I am all there is to that which is called elements...
composing that called weather.

I Am balance. My control is knowing I am balance, order, harmony; Because I am all these things it is the <u>only</u> activity going on.

The balance of knowing who I am looks like physical evidence.

I AM KNOWING THIS.

Because I Am Completeness,

Everything which includes my experience is complete.

To be good means to be right in every direction.

Perfectly balanced means to be the oneness and allness line of perfection, order, harmony.

IT IS ALL SELF REVELATION.

STATEMENTS ON BEING

I maintain the fact of my own completeness and perfection in the midst of all circumstance and there cannot be any circumstance contrary to what I know myself to be.

As will, genius, opportunity...
I utilize all my tools (inborn qualities).
As I think I am completeness, this includes all identity.
Completeness is the cause of being complete.
It is self revelation.
The nature of my Being is balanced being;
There cannot be too much or too little of any identity.

I am Thinker Thinking thought — there isn't thought and then some formation; thought IS the formation.

There are no delays, no gaps, only simultaneous, spontaneous Being!

Because I am infinity as Thinker Thinking, thought is infinite.

I cannot avoid the appearance of myself.
Thought is the appearance of Thinker Thinking.
It is co-instantaneous and constant-aneous.

In thinking, always have the order as: cause – effect. Always use, I (Mind, Soul, Spirit) Am...

Being who and what I Am, Thinker Thinking thought,
is right here – infinite,
right now – eternal.

I do not have to formulate or do anything — just be who and what I am. This looks like doing things. My quality of thought is my activity, my evidence of action.

STATEMENTS ON BEING

Because I maintain the fact of my own completeness and perfection in the midst of all circumstance, there cannot be any circumstance contrary to what I know myself to be.

My Premise includes qualities of thinking
I know myself to be.
Therefore my Conclusion has to be in accord with that,
or 'it can't be true'.

My self revelation speaks to me in the language of ideas and I recognize myself in those ideas.

All those qualities that I am are the facts about my ideas – so, therefore, all my ideas are complete, perfect, harmonious, orderly.
I don't need to think about what to do, or bring it about since they are of me and I am here, whole and complete.

Conceit and arrogance asks:
"Who do you think you are to get past me?"
I answer;
"I Am Consciousness and I Am All. You are nothing."
It all boils down to cause/effect.

As I see what I am not, right there it's telling me (serving me) that I know what I Am. That is its function. There is no time, space or process involved — it is just being...
positive/negative being.

There is only one mentality present. The Presence, Intelligence, Power and Action of good.
I AM IT!!
THIS IS IT!

Thinker Thinking moves thought.
Thought is all there is to person/body.

I can't know it all because it is infinite.
As consciousness, I am infinite.
I am Light – persistent, insistent, constant Light.

Declaring (qualifying) who, why, where, when, what, which, how I am dispels the false assumptions of darkness.

STATEMENTS ON BEING

Always think:
"I am all there is to that,"
NOT:
'That' is not all there is to me."

Effect is nothing in and of itself.

My identification, my world, can't be there without me.

Knowing this...
IS MY FULL TIME JOB!!

There are no opinions to me.
That is the constancy of it, like playing a beautiful melody.

That all this appears vast and unlimited is really
my identification.

I AM HERE AND NOW THE CONTINUAL
UNFOLDMENT OF BEING.

STATEMENTS ON BEING

My Is-ness is all that I consciously Am as Thinker Thinking. There is no presence, intelligence, power or action to anything other than my I-Am-Ness.

There is nothing appearing 'out there' to think back at me. What looks like 'out there' – person, place, thing, etc. – is evidence of me as Thinker Thinking thought.

In qualifying, sometimes there is the assumption you are
dealing with effect and trying to make it cause.
Don't start with a result.
Focus is the action of knowing who and what I Am.

My skill is to realize that cause is cause, effect is effect.
One cannot be without the other.

 STATEMENTS ON BEING

POSITIVE/NEGATIVE BEING

POSITIVE/NEGATIVE BEING

I Am Light and I cannot become darkness.
Darkness is unknowing.

Nothing is more simple than Oneness of The One.

STATEMENTS ON BEING

My I am-ness is Light.

I Am the full effulgence of Light which never dims.
There can be no element of myself as Light
which can be darkness.

I am the continuity of inspiration.

Light is present as my Self.
That is the Law of my Being.

I rejoice in my I Am-ness.

I am positive negative Being.

LIGHT

POSITIVE/NEGATIVE BEING

What I am not could not appear without what I Am.

What I am not has no independent presence, intelligence, power or action.

I know it is Not because I know what IS.

STATEMENTS ON BEING

My positive Being automatically implies
there is nothing else.

POSITIVE/NEGATIVE BEING

There is no self destructive element in myself as Consciousness.

I am positive/negative Being.

Atom is the evidence of me as Thinker Thinking.

STATEMENTS ON BEING

What I Am includes the inborn declaration of what I Am not. When I say I Am, this implies anything else is not.

Each individual identity is eternal and infinitely expressed.

In this room, all that's here is because of me;

I Am Light.

I don't <u>try</u> to be Light.

POSITIVE/NEGATIVE BEING

I'm not looking for anything,

I am expectant desire to see myself everywhere
and I am self recognition.

I will see and recognize myself everywhere and I will see who
and what I am NOT right here – but I don't have to
do anything to it.

Enthusiasm is self inspiration. It is myself as Light.

Enthusiasm and inspiration are sisters, inter-related.

POSITIVE/NEGATIVE BEING

The positive existence of myself is the negative non-existence of all I am not.

There is only one negative and that is the positive/negative of myself as Light;

The yes of my positive existence 'I' is an automatic 'no' to the possibility of anything else.

THERE IS NOT A SEPARATE NEGATIVE.

Seeing/thinking/recognizing that I am not what is appearing
IS the negative of my positive negative Being,
Being Light.

POSITIVE/NEGATIVE BEING

There is no 'is-not-ness' out there being annulled.

My I-Amness, the Universal State of Being IS Light.

DUALITY

STATEMENTS ON BEING

If it appears to be good and I have it 'out there' separate from myself as Consciousness, it IS NOT – It is nothing…

Regarding what looks like 'others':

'They' stand 'there' as self-aware Being –
that is 'their' reality, but –
I Am the awareness of that.

I Am That I Am...

STATEMENTS ON BEING

World thought tries to tell me I'm the offspring of duality, that I was born into it, struggle through it, then die in it.

That IS NOT my I-Am-ness.

DO NOT SUCCUMB IN IT!

Be the comforter of myself – I AM ALL.
I AM PERSON.
I AM MIND.
I AM THE WAY...Within-ness.
THE ONLY WAY.

DUALITY

It is right to know the nature of duality – but this does not make it real. I have to know the nothing-ness. Seeing it 'as it is' stops it. There is nothing else to do but 'see' the Truth of It, here and now.

Only habit keeps me going back.

STATEMENTS ON BEING

Worshipping something grand and glorious is 'two,' rather than BEING IT. There is One person and I Am identified in infinite variety.

It looks like other persons but there is no separation between 'I' appearing as person and person whomever.

Infinity is unfathomable.
I see more and more that I Am 'It'…
This eliminates martyrdom and self sacrifice.

I, Me, My, Mine, You, We, Us, Our – All who I Am.

If it appears that I am separate, assumption prevails.
Then that's what I am NOT.

DUALITY

Let go of trying to process, manipulate and control.

Stop trying to correct my thinking.
I am thinker qualifies my thinking.
Stop getting it 'out there.'

My image is inevitable — the effort to <u>make</u> it change is the sweat and struggle.

It is habit to go out there and explain something.

Duality is divisibility.

Don't look 'out there' at appearances to qualify oneself.

Assumption is always the function of duality, i.e., let us suppose, let us pretend - pretense.

Fate vs. Free Will is total duality.

Duality is always present as what is not.
I don't have to get rid of it.

The whole idea of having a choice humanly is totally not true. If I think I have a choice that's duality. If I think I have anything that's duality. There is only I Am all that is – nothing to get, only to be.

The nature of duality (evil) has to be understood or else it will appear to be what I Am.

It must be seen that that which appears to be…is not.
What is not? The assumption that it is separate from me.
It is either what I am or what I am not.
I qualify myself and it 'appears' as that…
It is NOT on it's own.

DUALITY

Thinking I have a body to move or not move — to be stiff, to be in or out of — is duality.

FALSE MENTALITY

FALSE MENTALITY

The duality of false mentality will always take an appearance of reality.

Ask oneself – did I originate that?
Did I say this is what I Am?

STATEMENTS ON BEING

Regarding false concepts and assumptions —
ask oneself...are they my I Am-ness?

FALSE MENTALITY

Self-analysis is the perversion of qualifying myself.
I don't have to justify who I Am.

To seek Light is error.

There is nothing external to me, Consciousness.
I don't have light – I Am Light.

FALSE MENTALITY

Philosophy is a theory of knowledge, speculations, super-fine pretense, and is ultimately superficial.

Going out to seek or find is what I am not.

I am infinity.

A sense of futility, helplessness, frustration in the 'task' of fixing anything has only to do with who and what I am NOT.

FALSE MENTALITY

I Am Consciousness.

I am not a pendulum.
I am not a victim.
I am not a sponge.
I am not a target.

ALL NOTHING BEING NOTHING.

STATEMENTS ON BEING

Conceit and arrogance are only false mentality,
a fabrication of itself.

There are no degrees of evil manifesting.
There are no layers.
There are no rings of hell mentally manifesting.

I Am the thinker mind and I do not create anything like that.

The assumption is that there is something other than me going on, putting on masks to dramatize nothing.

FALSE MENTALITY

Let go of the conceit of dramatizing, being on a white charger, parading around being a great person doing something great in life.
All the qualities that constitute my goals are going on right now, right here. Future tense is just the continuity and perpetuity of those qualities.
It is all self revelation.
I Am completeness.
I Am the thing itself.

STATEMENTS ON BEING

Duplicity, hypnosis, pretense, perversion, etc.
ALL is-not-ness.
Soul Self (my I Am-ness) bears testimony.
Eyes are doing the seeing and testifying.
Ears are hearing and testifying.

FALSE MENTALITY

What I am not cannot be thinking — just suggestions
coming from duality — what I Am Not!
I'm not a sponge.
I'm not a victim.
Nothing to do with me.
I am self sufficient being.
I am all that I ever will be or can be.
I am fullness of Being Here and Now.
How can there be more than All?

STATEMENTS ON BEING

If I am not it, then it is not. Knowing this is the is-not-ness.
I am not a receptacle. I don't have a consciousness.
I Am Consciousness.

EXERCISE:
Stand before the mirror, see my reflection, know that my identity is all I have put my 'I am-ness' to.
Something comes between my reflection and me, a mist or veil arises, appearing as either good or bad. This is the great deceiver. It appears as something separate from me.

KNOW:
This is only an assumption.

DO NOT RESPOND OR REACT!

I THAT IS WE

STATEMENTS ON BEING

Marriage is not two, it is One...an infinite count of One. Declare sovereign individuality.

As you see your universe is full of person, place, thing; all that is appearing has to appear as I know myself to be... complete, whole, satisfied.

I don't have to provide for, be for. My only obligation is to myself. I am not a martyr or self sacrificial.

I am independent by being the oneness and allness of Being.

I am grateful I know, love and honor myself through what I see as person, place or thing.

I am doing all AS myself, not _for_ myself.

When one sees correctly that anything/person appearing 'out there' is really oneself objectified, then you see you are still doing it as yourself.

STATEMENTS ON BEING

Golden Rule:
Treat another as myself because the other IS myself.

I am self care, self sustaining being.
I don't give of myself; that is being a martyr.
I'm just Being — it might look like giving, or...

In the one-ness of Being there is only One here.

I THAT IS WE

I am positively declaring there is nothing separate from myself – simultaneous Is-ness. My effect is what I see out there and it is complementary to me. It has to be as I Am. It is evidence of who, why, when, where, what, which, How I Am.

I outline myself. It is All myself.

Universal 'WE' is 'I, Consciousness'.

WHY AM I? – I AM because I Am – My purpose is to Be.

There is nothing preexistent to ME that can be the reason for My Existence; Nothing precedes ME, The Ultimate IS.

SO ALL THAT I CONSCIOUSLY AM ESSENTIALLY IS!

PAST PRESENT FUTURE

STATEMENTS ON BEING

In the infinitude of my Being as infinity, there has never been a moment of chaos. I am order – the right thing done at the right time in the right way.

I am balanced being.
Every element of my being is in perfect balance.

Don't limit here and now – past and future ARE Here, Now.

False assumptions/false mentality claims priority through history. I qualify myself here and now. I am all there is to past and future – Here and now.

STATEMENTS ON BEING

NOW,

I am perfection, purity, completeness, harmony, order, beauty,
eternity, infinity, affluence and health.
I do honor the qualities of myself that come full circle
and are here now as I am Here now.

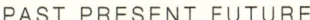 PAST PRESENT FUTURE

The present is all there is to the past. It goes frontwards and backwards — perpetual — infinite.

Faces may change but qualities endure.
Individual identity is eternal.

CPSIA information can be obtained
at www.ICGtesting.com
Printed in the USA
BVHW041946100323
660182BV00006B/375